OUTDOOR ADVENTURE

TURKEY HUNTING

BY GEORGE PENDERGAST

Gareth Stevens
PUBLISHING

HOT TOPICS

Please visit our website, www.garethstevens.com. For a free color catalog of all our high-quality books, call toll free 1-800-542-2595 or fax 1-877-542-2596.

Pendergast, George.
Turkey hunting / by George Pendergast.
p. cm. — (Outdoor adventure)
Includes index.
ISBN 978-1-4824-1268-0 (pbk.)
ISBN 978-1-4824-1238-3 (6-pack)
ISBN 978-1-4824-1494-3 (library binding)
1. Turkey hunting — Juvenile literature. I. Title.
SK325.T8 P46 2015
799.2—d23

First Edition

Published in 2015 by
Gareth Stevens Publishing
111 East 14th Street, Suite 349
New York, NY 10003

Designer: Nick Domiano
Editor: Ryan Nagelhout

Photo credits: Cover, p. 1 Jeff Banke/Shutterstock.com; cover texture Yuriy Boyko/Shutterstock.com; cover ribbon blinkblink/Shutterstock.com; pp. 4-5 kzww/Shutterstock.com; pp. 6-7 Tom Reichner/Shutterstock.com; pp. 8-9, 14-15 Bruce MacQueen/Shutterstock.com; pp. 10-11 Sandy Hedgepeth/Shutterstock.com; p. 13 Dewayne Flowers/ Shutterstock.com; p. 17 Stephen Simpson/The Image Bank/Getty Images; pp. 18-19, 24-25 Bryan Eastham/Shutterstock.com; p. 21 Michael Pearce/Wichita Eagle/Getty Images; pp. 22-23, 28-29 Brent Frazee/Kansas City Star/Getty Images; pp. 26-27 Bree Richards/Shutterstock.com; p. 30 (bow) Andrey_Popov/Shutterstock.com; p. 30 (gun) zimand/Shutterstock.com.

Printed in the United States of America

CPSIA compliance information: Batch #CS15GS: For further information contact Gareth Stevens, New York, New York at 1-800-542-2595.

CONTENTS

TURKEY HUNT

Hunting is lots of fun! There are many places you can go to hunt different animals. One great animal to hunt is the turkey.

Turkeys are large birds. They have long necks and many feathers. They have a big organ in their neck called a **gizzard**. The gizzard is very strong. It helps wild turkeys eat almost anything!

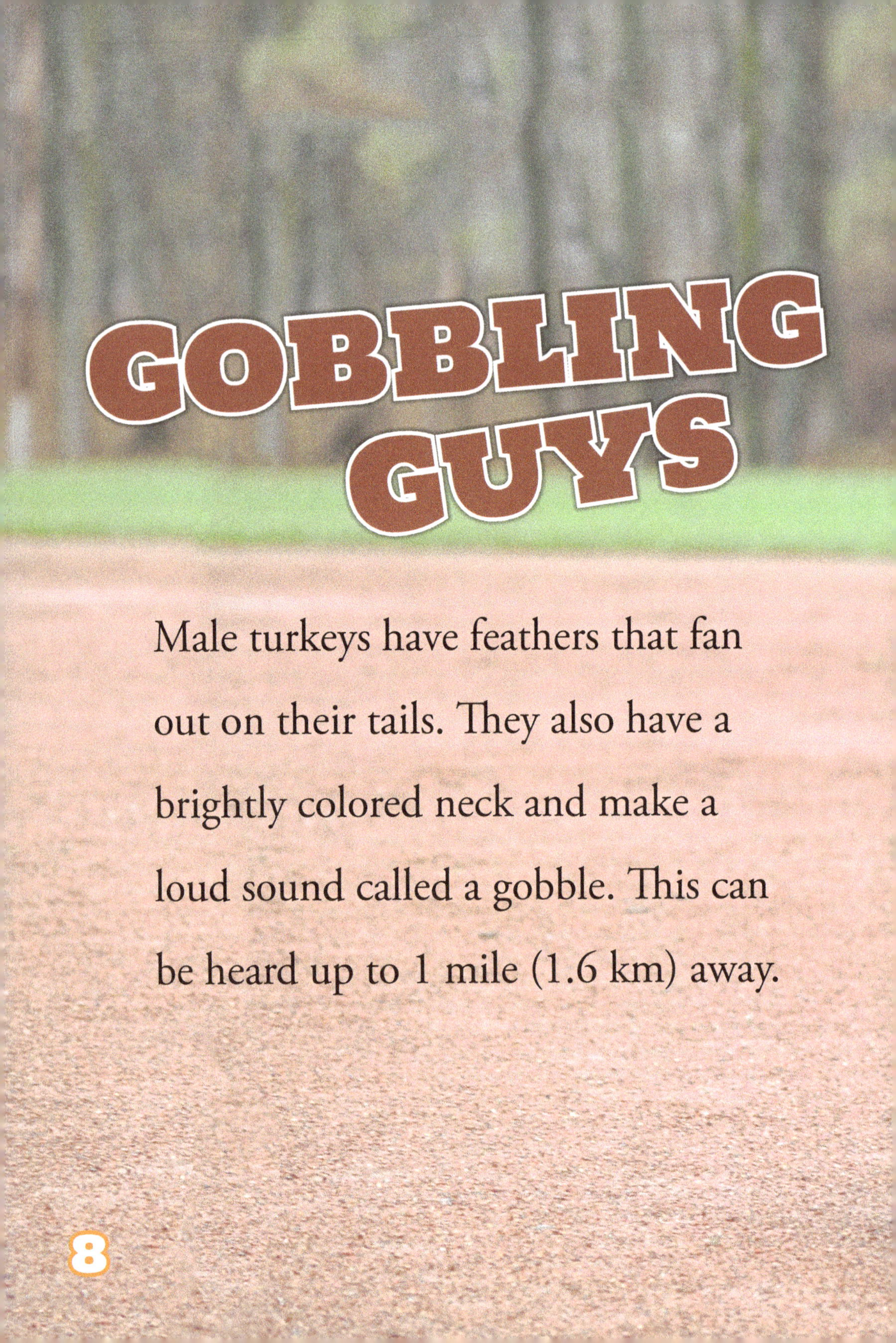

GOBBLING GUYS

Male turkeys have feathers that fan out on their tails. They also have a brightly colored neck and make a loud sound called a gobble. This can be heard up to 1 mile (1.6 km) away.

Different kinds of turkeys live throughout North America. Eastern turkeys live on the East Coast. Osceola turkeys live in Florida. There are also turkeys in other parts of the world, even Hawaii and New Zealand!

Hunters use different kinds of **weapons** to hunt turkeys. Some people use a bow and arrow to shoot the turkey. Others use a type of gun called a shotgun, which uses shells or bullets.

HUNTING SEASONS

People hunt turkeys in the spring and fall. The periods you're allowed to hunt are called seasons. Most seasons are based on the type of weapon you use on the hunt. Different states have different dates for their turkey hunting seasons.

Each state has special rules about hunting wild turkeys. Some states let younger hunters start their season early. This lets young hunters gain experience and have a better chance to bag a bird!

Turkey hunters need cover to avoid scaring turkeys away. Some hunters use **blinds** they build near open fields. Others hide in wooded areas or **brush** where the birds can't see them. While turkeys look for food in fields, hunters try to bring them close to their hiding spot.

DECOYS AND CALLS

Hunters use fake turkeys, called decoys, to attract the birds to an area. Decoys can look like different kinds of turkeys. Hunters stick the decoys in the ground and try to get the turkeys' attention.

Getting turkeys to come toward hunters takes more than decoys. Hunters also use a call to **mimic** the sounds a turkey makes. Hunters listen to the gobbles of a wild turkey and use different calls to sound just like them!

TAKING THE SHOT

Once a turkey gets close, hunters can take their shot. If they miss, it's best to wait for birds to come back later. Hunters don't want to scare turkeys away from their hiding spots!

Turkey hunters use as much of the bird as they can. Many people mount the tail of the turkey they get. They spread the feathers out to make a fan. They also use the turkey as food.

Turkey hunting is a great way to learn about nature. You have to study wild turkeys to know how to hunt them. Get outside and start planning your own turkey hunt with your family.

TURKEY HUNTING SAFETY

- Never move decoys that aren't covered up by something.
- Always act as if every gun or bow is loaded.
- Never point a gun or bow at anyone.
- Don't put your finger on a gun or bow's trigger until you're ready to fire.
- Be sure of your target before firing.
- Always wear orange so other hunters can see you.

FOR MORE INFORMATION

Books

Green, Sara. *Turkey Hunting*. Minneapolis, MN: Bellwether Media, 2014.

Lambert, Hines. *Hunting Turkeys*. New York, NY: Powerkids Press, 2013.

Omoth, Tyler. *Turkey Hunting for Kids*. North Mankato, MN: Capstone Press, 2013

Websites

Turkey Hunting

fieldandstream.com/hunting/birds/turkeys

Find articles and get answers to questions at the Field & Stream turkey-hunting site.

Turkey Hunting Tips and Tactics

nwtf.org/for_hunters/hunting_tactics.html

Get great tips and tricks from the National Wild Turkey Federation to help you snag a turkey.

Publisher's note to educators and parents: Our editors have carefully reviewed these websites to ensure that they are suitable for students. Many websites change frequently, however, and we cannot guarantee that a site's future contents will continue to meet our high standards of quality and educational value. Be advised that students should be closely supervised whenever they access the Internet.

GLOSSARY

blind: a small building hunters hide in while they watch for animals

brush: short trees or bushes

gizzard: a large tubelike muscle in a bird's throat that helps them break down food

mimic: to make the same sound as something else

weapon: something used to injure or kill

INDEX